This Journal belongs to

_____

"Seek the wisdom that will untie your knot.
Seek the path that demands your whole being." Rumi

Welcome to Your Happiness Journal

May this Happiness Journal be an invitation and an opportunity for you to adventure into a new chapter of your life. In an increasingly uncertain world, it is precisely our ability to open up new pathways that enables us to be "the light" both for ourselves and those around us.

Happiness Journal has been conceived as a chance to create a quiet thoughtful space in your life so that you can reconnect with Nature through sensory discovery, open up your creativity and enable healing through drawing. Happiness Journal is based on the unique "friendship" of three main elements which together will help you experience yourself in a totally different way.

First, the Journal introduces Nature's luxurious gifts of essential oils to your daily reflection activities. Did you know that your sense of smell is the most powerful of your senses, and probably the most neglected one too? Added to a daily mindfulness practice of being present in the moment with kindness and curiosity, the aroma of these purest of essences can be a powerful tool for reaching happiness. Smelling an essential oil while journaling and reflecting on the thoughts and feelings it triggers for you is an invaluable step towards knowing what your soul truly needs, as well as allowing healing to happen.

Secondly, the Journal invites you to explore a new visual language that can help transform your thinking and therefore reinvent your life. It is called Neurographica® and when you learn to use it well, you can make your dreams come true simply by drawing them.

Thirdly, writing by hand has amazing benefits for your brain - it engages it on a deeper level. As we write by hand, we slow down allowing ideas to form and come to the surface of our awareness.

Over the following days, as you get to experience the essential oils on a much deeper level, and as you begin to draw Neurographica, I invite you to connect with your body, heart and mind and see how they respond to the environment around you but most importantly, focus on the relationship you have with yourself. As you go through the Journal, in just 10 min a day, you will become much more deeply connected to your true self, you will get to know yourself better and you will fall in love with the special Soul that lives inside your body.

The combined effect of thoughtful contemplation, Neurographica drawing and the amazing aromas of essential oils will deepen your awareness, inspire insights and empower your choices in life. Do it just for you and begin to uncover the wisdom that lives within.

Wishing you insightful reflections,

Desi Stefanova

 To provide yourself with the optimum benefit, it is recommended that you use the highest possible grade of essential oils. If you don't have these oils yet, drop me an email at contact@DesiStefanova.com

Contents:

Before You Begin

What are Essential Oils?

Essential oils are the essence of a plant, a gift from the earth, distilled and prepared for us so we can bring the power of Nature into our homes.

Inside many plants, hidden in their roots, stems, seeds, flowers, leaves and bark, are concentrated, highly potent natural aromatic chemical compounds (tiny organic molecules), called essential oils. There are no wasted efforts in Nature and so the fragrance of a flower, the smell of an orange, the scent of a pine tree, all serve a specific purpose vital for the plant's survival. When we experience an essential oil, we are in fact utilising that plant's medicine for our benefit. There are over 3,000 different aromatic constituents and they are all around us. The cells of our body recognise them because they "speak the same language".

Apart from helping the physical body in times when modern science doesn't always have solutions to deal with new evolving pathogens, essential oils are here to guide us through periods of emotional, mental or spiritual challenges so we can reclaim our birthright of happiness, health, vitality, emotional and mental harmony and spiritual awakening.

"It doesn't get much greener than essential oils: when used correctly, they are among Mother Nature's most potent remedies."
Amy Leigh Mercree

Essential oils are very powerful. They are 50-70 times more potent than the complete plant. To put this into perspective, one drop of Peppermint essential oil can have the same impact on the body as 28 cups of peppermint tea, according to research.

Remember this when using essential oils:

they are very concentrated!

How to Use the Oils

Ensuring the maximum potency and beneficial properties of an essential oil is the result of maintaining the delicate ratio of the aromatic compounds found in that oil, all of which can vary depending on the time and part of the plant which is harvested, the time of the year or life cycle when harvested, the geographic location and weather where the plant was grown, or the method and even the duration of distillation. For that reason, it is vital that the essential oils you use come from a trusted source committed to not only producing unadulterated (uncontaminated) essential oils but also to adhering to the strictest production protocols. There are no wasted efforts in Nature, and neither should there be in the healthcare you provide for yourself and those you love.

When using essential oils, always follow the safety guidelines of the company which produced them.

Aromatic Use (Breath)

Each time you inhale, you breathe in oxygen and the life force gifted to you from the surrounding plants and trees. As you exhale, you gift in return carbon dioxide which the plants and trees need for their survival. It becomes a symbiotic relationship between humans and plants: your exhale is the plants' inhale, your inhale is their exhale.

Inhaling an essential oil can have an amazing and fast impact on your whole body. Through the lungs, the aromatic compounds enter the bloodstream. At the same time, they communicate with your olfactory system (your sense of smell) to influence the parts of your brain known as the limbic system- your brain's emotional control centre and the place where your memories are created and stored. As a result, oils alter the physiological functions throughout your entire body.

"Smell is a potent wizard that transports you across thousand of miles and all the years you have lived."
Helen Keller

Nothing takes you down memory lane faster than your sense of smell. As you inhale an essential oil, it impacts your mind, your emotions, your memories and your body follows along with the corresponding physiology: uplifting and energizing, calming and grounding, or anything else in between. Breath by breath, you transmute what needs healing so you can move forward. The oils work fast, modulating your emotions within seconds.

Topical Use (Skin)

When applying essential oils on the skin, they are quickly absorbed into the bloodstream and travel around your body. For topical use it is always wise to dilute the essential oils in what is known as a carrier oil, such as coconut oil. This serves two main goals: it ensures absorption (the coconut oil "carries" the essential oil through the skin reducing the amount of evaporation) and it prevents any possible skin sensitivity or irritation.

Start with 1 drop of essential oil and 10 drops of carrier oil and do a small "patch test". Apply a little bit on the inner forearm and if there is no reaction after a few hours, you can feel comfortable applying the essential oil in that dilution everywhere else on the body. With time and experience, you will know how your body reacts to different dilution ratios. If your skin begins to turn red, to itch or burn after applying an oil, remove the oil by gently wiping the area with a soft cloth, then alternate between adding a carrier oil and gently wiping the area.

 Never apply essential oils inside the nose, the inner ear, the eyes, on broken skin or on other sensitive areas (e.g. genitals).

Internal Use (Ingesting)

Pure essential oils can be taken internally for a number of benefits. All you need is a drop or two at a time. You can add the oil to water, another drink or place in an empty capsule and swallow. When taken internally, essential oils have many benefits. They support the immune system and its function, aid the respiratory system, help the body obtain antioxidants to protect against free radical damage, support the normal digestive process, ease indigestion and occasional stomach upset. They also help the heart (your body's hardest working organ) and the whole circulatory system that transports oxygen, nutrients, hormones and waste throughout the body, every moment of every day. When ingested, essential oils cleanse all internal body systems and calm the nervous system with better sleep, vital nutrients, exercise support and calming the nerves.

What is Neurographica?

Neurographica® is a relatively new method of transforming our reality using paper, pens and colouring pencils. It was created by the Russian psychologist, architect and philosopher Pavel Piskarev. The name "Neuro-Graphica" has two Latin roots: "neuro" (the interconnected neurones in the brain) and "graphica" (drawing connected shapes and lines on various life topics).

Neurographica is a simple concept with a lot of science behind it. While drawing on paper, you heal inside. The Artist (You) is the most important part in Neurographica. How you feel and what you think while drawing has preference over what you are drawing. Consider it as a kind of Art Meditation to explore your subconscious behavioural patterns, express your emotions, activate your creativity and open up hidden potential. It is a very simple and beautiful method to transform reality.

How to Use This Journal

The rule is that there is no rule. There is no right or wrong way to journal- there is only YOUR WAY. If you are new to journaling, the following suggestions may be useful.

1) Do one prompt/page per day, going through the Journal as suggested. You may find that you like certain prompts more than others and you may feel strong resistance to doing some. You can certainly choose to avoid focusing on the prompts you don't like because this is your Journal. You can skip those and never think about them again or you could return to them at a later day when it feels more natural to you. You could even change them if you want. It's your journal. You decide how best to use it.

2) Before you "meet" the oil for the day, settle into a comfortable position, close your eyes and focus on your breathing. Gently, without judgment, begin to notice how you are feeling in this moment.

> *Is your body tense or relaxed?*
> *Are there any particular spots of tension (shoulders, neck)?*
> *What is your emotional state?*

3) Open the essential oil bottle and start inhaling the aroma. You can even put a drop in your palms, shape them into a cup and inhale. Do it mindfully, giving yourself time to honour both the essential oil and yourself. As you do this, focus your attention on the aroma and any other sensations that are happening for you right now.

> *What colour or shape would you associate with the aroma that is now filling your nose, your lungs, your brain, your whole body?*
> *Are there any memories or recollections that you can associate with this particular scent?*
> *How would you describe the way you are feeling in this moment?*

4) Reflect on the experience by recording the thoughts and memories that came to you. If words are powerless to convey the feeling, you could always draw images and ideas.

5) Check out the short description of the oil.

> *Do you agree with the description?*
> *Were you able to notice similar changes/shifts to your emotional state during this mindful exercise?*

6) Each essential oil section is in a different colour and includes a Neurographica activity. It is best to do these in order starting from Step 1 and gradually learn the basics. Additional resources are available in the Art Studio (see page 96) so it won't be long before you start drawing meaningful, life-transformative pictures.
https://www.DesiStefanova.com/Journal

If at any moment, it becomes uncomfortable, take a break from the scent and focus on your breathing.

Happiness Goals

The practice of mindful awareness can help reduce worry, uplift mood, and promote feelings of regained focus and productivity. Combined with essential oils, increasing your awareness of yourself and your surroundings can help you to slow down and feel more relaxed during an increasingly busy life.

Using the space on the next pages, set yourself some "Happiness Goals". If you need initial help, the prompts will get you going. Ignore them if you already know what you want to achieve.
You can revisit these goals regularly to check on your progress or to amend them. As you grow and develop, so will your goals.

Have fun and enjoy!

"Watch and witness. Your body is not you; your mind is not you. You are just a pure witness." Osho

Prompts:

My top 3 priorities right now are...

This isn't working in my life right now, so...

My life needs more...

The things that make me happy are...

I always love doing...

My Happiness Goals:

"The fears we don't face become our limits." Robin Sharma

Lavender
Lavandula angustifolia

Relax, Nurture, Calm, Soothe;
Openness, Honest Contemplation

If you are looking for ways to deepen your connection with Nature, then this can be your helping tool.

Usage Tips:

- Add Lavender to an evening bath to soak away the cares of the day.
- Put a drop on your pillow at night for restful sleep and diffuse Lavender oil at bedtime to calm your mind and create a peaceful environment. (Diffusers disperse the oil without heating it.)
- Take internally to reduce anxious feelings.
- Freshen your linen closet, mattress, car or the air by combining Lavender with water in a spray bottle.
- Keep a bottle of Lavender oil on hand to soothe occasional skin irritations.

 For safe ingestion, only use oils that are guaranteed free from harmful chemicals (pesticides, solvents, fillers, and other impurities). Bear in mind that bottle labels can be misleading.

The scent of Lavender oil reminds me of...

As you sit quietly, notice each breath you
take. Follow the intake of air with Lavender oil
through your nose into your lungs and the slow
exhalation as you release the air through your
nose. Repeat this mindful breathing for several
minutes and notice how your body feels...

I pause, rest and just observe...

Did You Know: It takes 3 pounds of Lavender flowers and leaves to produce just one 15mL bottle of pure Lavender essential oil.

I'm not spending enough energy on...

I'm spending too much energy on...

If Nature could speak, it would say that ...

Check out the Neurographica drawing inspired by Lavender on the page 12 where you can see lots of wiggly lines. They are called Neurographic Lines (or Neurolines for short). A Neuroline does not repeat itself in any segment of its way, and it goes where you don't expect to see it. There are a lot of these lines in Nature.

Go in Nature and breathe in your Lavender oil. The smell of Lavender will help you discover the comfort and serenity that your soul craves.

While there, see if you can spot any Neurolines.

An interesting new discovery: let's draw!

Step 1 - The Neuroline

Neurolines are at the heart of Neurographica. A Neuroline never repeats and always goes where you don't expect to see it. Neurolines are very much Nature-like. Have you seen any such lines on your nature walks? In road or wall cracks, the lines of ocean waves, the outlines of clouds, the crowns of trees or the paths of rivers on a map, Neurolines are everywhere. And now, would you like to draw some?

Drawing Neurolines could be a very interesting experience because the process requires you to move outside of pre-established patterns. While drawing Neurolines, watch your emotional state. Observe yourself: How are you feeling? Are you surprised by your actions? Are you excited by change, by opportunities life brings? Or does change cause you stress?

This simple drawing activity alone can tell you a lot about yourself. You can find a video demonstration and further tips in the Art Studio.

https://www.DesiStefanova.com/Journal

Peppermint
Mentha piperita

Awaken, Revitalise, Cool, Digest;
Uplifting, Inspiring Action

If you feel confused, heavy or hopeless, this is your tool to blow away the clouds of doubt and despair.

Usage Tips:

- Take one to two drops of Peppermint essential oil in a veggie capsule to alleviate occasional stomach upset.
- Add a drop to your favorite smoothie recipe for a refreshing twist.
- Use a drop of Peppermint with Lemon in water for a healthy, refreshing mouth rinse.
- Place one drop in palm of hand with one drop Lemon and one drop Frankincense and inhale for a mid-day pick-me-up.

When I smell Peppermint I think of...

As you sit quietly, notice each breath you take. Follow the intake of air with Peppermint oil through your nose into your lungs and the slow exhalation as you release the air through your nose. Repeat this mindful breathing for several minutes and notice how your body feels...

I feel happiest when...

How do I celebrate the joy of being alive?

I'd like to have more of these positive thoughts...

Neurolines and Peppermint oil: I observe...

What thoughts and memories does Peppermint oil trigger in your mind?

Step 2 - Practice drawing some Neurolines.

As a thought comes along, let your hand move the pen across the page, slowly and mindfully, engaging in that thought and being curious about it. When another thought comes, draw another Neuroline. It doesn't matter if the lines cross. There is a short video lesson on this Step in the Art Studio:

https://www.DesiStefanova.com/Journal

Draw as many Neurolines as you like. You could even experiment with speed (draw slower, then draw faster) and you could even change hands. Be curious. Observe. Notice.

When you think you have finished, look at your drawing and consider:

How is this picture a reflection of your reality and your life? Are there any repeated patterns? Were the lines more interesting when you drew slowly? What does that mean for you?

Share your discoveries in the Online community and read other people's observation.

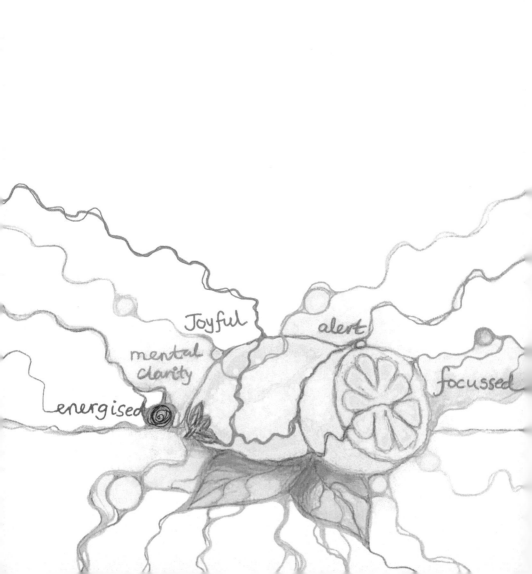

Lemon

Citrus limon

Cleanse, Detox, Focus:
Energy, Joy, Happiness

If you are constantly thinking limiting thoughts and you need more light in your life, introduce Lemon essential oil to your day.

Usage Tips:

- Diffuse to create an uplifting environment.
- Add one drop of Lemon essential oil to a glass of water for a refreshing drink that aids digestion and naturally cleanses the body.
- Add Lemon Essential Oil to a spray bottle of water to clean tables, counter-tops, and other surfaces.
- For a gentle furniture polish, simply add a few drops of Lemon to olive oil on a cloth to clean, protect and shine wood finishes.
- Wipe down stainless steel appliances with a soft cloth soaked in Lemon oil for a streak-free clean.

 Lemon essential oil comes from the rind of the fruit and is totally different from lemon juice.

Avoid exposure to direct sunlight after topical use of Lemon oil because it may cause the skin to burn more easily.

Lemon oil scent reminds me of...

As you sit quietly, notice each breath you take. Follow the intake of air with Lemon oil through your nose into your lungs and the slow exhalation as you release the air through your nose. Repeat this mindful breathing for several minutes and notice how your body feels...

What most excites me and ignites my passion is...

Did You Know: In one year, a single lemon tree has the potential to produce between 500 and 600 pounds of lemons. It typically takes around 75 lemons to fill a 15mL essential oil bottle.

Lemon essential oil is great for cooking, baking,, smoothies and cocktails. When taking essential oils internally, the quality and purity are extremely important! Make sure you trust the source of your oils before you ingest them.

When I was a kid, I loved (doing)...

Neurographica is a tool for self-discovery and
conscious modelling of dreams and goals.
Do you believe you can achieve your dreams?

I have this current Challenge in my life...

Inhale Lemon oil, imagine its golden light
flooding your entire body. Breathe deeply and
sit with the Challenge. Be curious: why it is here?
What do you need to learn from it?

Dispersing the Old, creating the New...

What would your Neurolines look like today, inspired by Lemon essential oil, on coloured paper? As you put your pen on the page, feel where you want your hand to go, but mindfully make a slight movement in the opposite direction. As you do that, you begin to break and change old patterns and habits.

Step 3 - "Rounding the corners"

Every time two Neurolines cross, they create four V-shaped corners at their intersection. Corners and pointy objects traditionally represent conflict, challenge and danger, while round and smooth objects represent harmony and balance. A key skill in Neurographica is the so called "rounding" or smoothing of the corners. As we round the V shapes to turn them into U shapes, we symbolically train our brain/mind to transform the conflict into harmony, making a soft transition from one line to another.

Now I invite you to go back to your previous drawings with Neurolines and practice rounding all the corners. Then you can draw some more Neurolines here and round the corners.

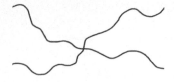

Neurolines cross and create sharp corners.

Round and smooth corners.

A short video tutorial is available in Art Studio. Check it out at:

https://www.DesiStefanova.com/Journal

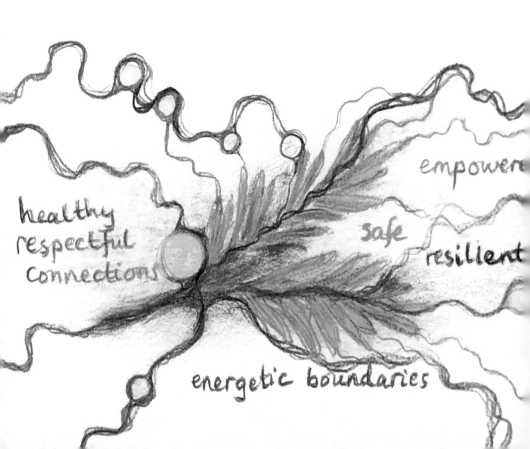

Tea Tree
Melaleuca

Healing, Mothering,;
Cleansing, Energetic Boundaries

If you are looking to heal your relationship with your mother (or women in general), or if you want to transform abundance issues by balancing your heart to be open to give as well as receive, then this is your helping tool.

Usage Tips:

· For skin irritations, apply 1-2 drops of Tea Tree essential oil onto the affected area.

· Combine 1-2 drops with your facial cleanser for added cleansing properties or apply to skin after shaving.

· Apply to fingernails and toenails after showering to purify and keep nails looking healthy.

· Add a few drops to a spray bottle with water and use on surfaces as a cleansing and purifying agent.

When I smell Tea Tree oil I think of...

As you sit quietly, notice each breath you take. Follow the intake of air with Tea Tree oil through your nose into your lungs and the slow exhalation as you release the air through your nose. Repeat this mindful breathing for several minutes and notice how your body feels...

Checking in with my Heart today...

Inhale Tea Tree, focus and listen within.
How are you feeling?

Did You Know: With over 92 different compounds, Tea Tree oil possesses almost endless wellness benefits. Bungawalbin Creek in Australia is surrounded by Australian Tea Trees and is held sacred by the Aboriginal and Torres Strait Islander peoples. As the sticky Tea Tree leaves fall into the creek, they create waters that natives still consider "magical waters" today.

Connecting with my Intuition

1. Choose an essential oil. Allow yourself to be drawn to one. Maybe Tea Tree?
2. Write down a question that has been bothering you recently.
3. Swap hands and start writing the answers with your non-dominant hand. It will be slower and harder because your mind will be focusing on letter formation.
4. And here is the trick! While the conscious mind is busy with letter formation, your intuition can come through freely, unfiltered, and it might surprise you with its wisdom.

   When you look at your answers, do not judge them, only learn from them.

"Everything in the Universe is within you. Ask all from yourself." Rumi

I deserve to be nurtured and loved.

Neurographica is a type of art that creates unique, seemingly abstract drawings. It doesn't matter how old you are, where you are in the world and it doesn't matter if you can or cannot draw because you don't have to be an artist to do it. None of this will affect your results. It's simple and it's easy! And it works for everyone!

As you inhale Tea Tree, notice your thoughts and begin to draw Neurolines - one for each thought that pops in your mind. Don't analyze these thoughts too much, just "empty" them on the paper. Then round the corners where the "thoughts" cross. Notice your feelings throughout.

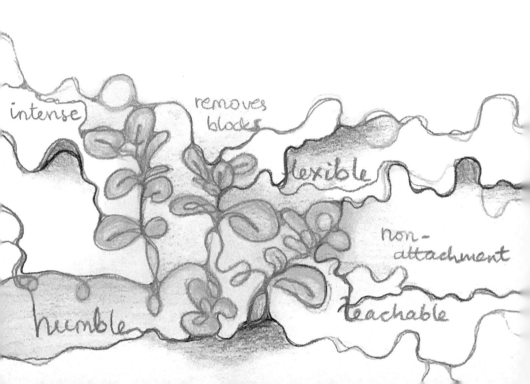

intense

removes
blocks

flexible

non-
attachment

teachable

humble

Oregano

Origanum vulgare

Immune, Respiratory, Digestive Support,
Straightforward, Unapologetic

If you are looking to let go of rigid beliefs and negative materialistic attachments (e.g. a destructive habit, a toxic relationship or an oppressive job) which hinder your growth and progress, then this is your helping tool.

Usage Tips:

- Taken internally, Oregano essential oil supports the digestive, respiratory, and immune systems. It's most popularly used for immune support. It offers powerful antioxidants. Oregano promotes the secretion of digestive juices. You can take Oregano internally by adding a few drops to water, taking it in a veggie capsule, or using it in recipes.

- Put one drop in place of 1 tablespoonful of dried oregano in spaghetti sauce, pizza sauce or on roast. For smaller amounts, dip a toothpick in the bottle, stir in the dish, taste and repeat if more needed.

Oregano is a one of the hottest oils and should always be diluted with a carrier oil such as fractionated coconut oil.

The scent of Oregano reminds me of...

As you sit quietly, notice each breath you
take. Follow the intake of air with Oregano oil
through your nose into your lungs and the slow
exhalation as you release the air through your
nose. Repeat this mindful breathing for several
minutes and notice how your body feels...

What areas of my life need a good clean?

Where plants grow is important for the quality of the essential oil they produce. Even the slightest change in the environment, e.g. climate, humidity, levels of sunlight, type of soil, geographic location, etc, can create totally different essential oil chemistry.

Reflect on your own environment. Your environment is created by internal and external forces. We can't always influence the external factors, but we can certainly do something about our internal dialogue.

The negative thought I have all the time that I'd like to change is...

Did You Know: The word "oregano" is derived from the Greek phrase "joy of the mountains".

It takes approximately 1 pound of oregano leaves to make 15mL of pure Oregano essential oil.

What does being humble mean to me?

Everyone has the right to have their own opinion and all opinions are valid. Do you agree?

Inhaling Oregano oil can support you in shifting any rigid belief that isn't serving your growth.

Where in my life do I experience rigidity?

Neurographica is based on your brain's plasticity and its ability to change at any age.

As you ponder the question, begin to draw Neurolines. The more Neurolines you draw, the more benefits you will experience. Then round the corners to soften the "stress" and achieve more fluid transfer of energy from one line through to the other.

Step 4 - "Adding colour"

Once all corners have been rounded, begin to colour in the shapes. The rule here is this: at least two neighbouring cells should be coloured in the same colour. You can also leave cells white because white is also a colour in Neurogrphica. A short video lesson is available in Art Studio. Feel free to check it out here: https://www.DesiStefanova.com/Journal

When you are ready, share your picture in the Online community.

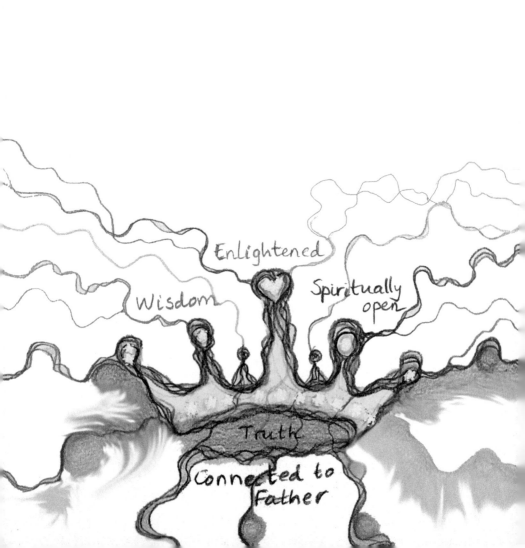

Frankincense

Boswellia carterii, frereana, and sacra

Healthy Immune and Brain Function;
Calming and Stabilising.

Frankincense gives us its essence when the tree is wounded, teaching us that we serve the world best as we experience and overcome times of hardship and danger.

Usage Tips:

- Rub Frankincense on your hands after a long day of gardening for a warming and soothing effect.
- Dilute and apply topically to reduce the appearance of skin imperfections.
- Apply to the bottom of feet to promote feelings of relaxation and to balance mood.
- Take one to two drops internally in a veggie capsule to support healthy cellular function.

 If in doubt, use Frank!

The smell of Frankincense reminds me of...

As you sit quietly, notice each breath you take. Follow the intake of air with Frankincense oil through your nose into your lungs and the slow exhalation as you release the air through your nose. Repeat this mindful breathing for several minutes and notice how your body feels...

How do I feel about being vulnerable?

"The difficult thing is that vulnerability is the first thing I look for in you and the last thing I'm willing to show you. In you, it's courage and daring. In me, it's weakness." Brene Brown

Did You Know: The "Frankincense" tree, known as Boswellia tree, can produce a couple of pounds of resin each year. If Boswellia trees are properly cared for, they can produce resin for hundreds of years. It takes approximately half a pound of resin to make 15mL bottle of Frankincense essential oil.

Checking in with the Divine Masculine

Our society has twisted the Divine Masculine aspect of Nature to mean aggressive, bossy and dominating behaviour. However, the Divine Masculine has many other facets such as protector, provider, creator.

It is vital to remember that the Divine Masculine is present within each of us. He brings the gifts of wisdom, confidence and analytical thinking.

To balance the Masculine, ponder the following questions. If you become uncomfortable at any time, smell Frankincense and let it transmute all negativity that no longer serves you.

What are my key beliefs about the Masculine?

What qualities of the Masculine do I admire?

What upsets me around the Masculine?

Do I really take responsibility for my life?

"The wound is the place where the Light enters you." Rumi

I am the best version of myself when I...

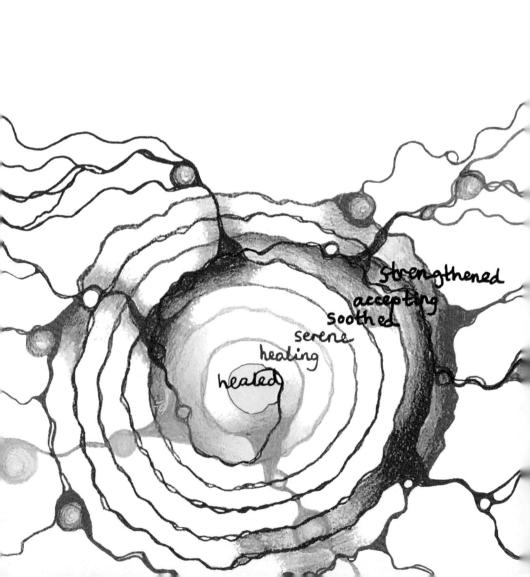

strengthened
accepting
soothed
serene
healing
healed

Soothing Blend

~~Wintergreen, Camphor,~~ Peppermint, ~~Ylang Ylang,
Helichrysum, Blue Tansy,~~ Blue Chamomile, and
~~Osmanthus~~ essential oils.

Myrr, (Mother Earth
oil. ♡)

Relief of Physical Pain;
Transformation and Healing of Underlying Emotional Cause

Much like peeling the layers of an onion, this blend will help you
uncover the message of the physical pain that you experience.

Usage Tips:

· Dilute with carrier oil to minimize any skin sensitivity during
  massage.

· Apply on feet and knees before and after exercise.

· Massage with a few drops of carrier oil onto growing kids' legs
  before bedtime.

· Rub on lower back muscles after a day of heavy lifting at work or
  after gardening.

Aromatic or Topical use only.

The scent of this blend reminds me of...

As you sit quietly, notice each breath you take. Follow the intake of air with Soothing blend through your nose into your lungs and the slow exhalation as you release the air through your nose. Repeat this mindful breathing for several minutes and notice how your body feels...

If my Body could speak, it would tell me...

"These pains you feel are messengers. Listen to them." Rumi

I love my Body because...

The main compounds of Wintergreen oil have long been known to science for their pain-soothing properties and are widely, and easily, produced synthetically to add to pain-relieving creams and ointments. They are cheap to make in a lab and easy to brand for profit, but less efficient and with side effects, unlike the real natural thing.

I need to be truthful with myself about...

"Nothing ever goes away until it has taught us what we need to know." Pema Chodron

Circles drawing meditation.

Step 5a - Circles

The "language" of Neurographica consists of Neurolines, circles, squares and triangles. They have different meaning and purpose. Circles are harmonising and bring tranquility, induce bliss and elevate us. Drawing circles on complicated topics helps to calm the mind and body. Drawing circles on purpose is akin to meditating.

As you begin to draw circles, notice the direction you prefer: clockwise or anticlockwise? See if you could change the direction and notice how that feels. Is it easier or harder?

When you have finished, look back at your drawing and ask yourself:

"How does this drawing represent my life? "
"How do I feel when I look at my drawing? "
"Are my circles too scattered or too close together?" "Do I need to make any changes to my drawing?"

A short video is available to demonstrate this activity. You can find it in Art Studio, here: https://www.DesiStefanova.com/Journal

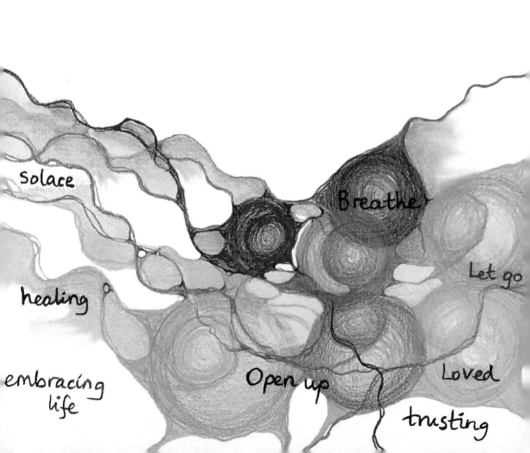

solace

Breathe

Let go

healing

embracing
life

Open up

Loved

trusting

Air
Respiratory Blend

~~Laurel Leaf~~, *Eucalyptus Leaf*, ~~Peppermint Plant~~,
Tea Tree Leaf, Lemon Peel, ~~Cardamom Seed~~,
~~Ravintsara Leaf, Ravensara Leaf~~ *essential oils.*

Lemon eucalyptus,
Celery seed, spearmint

Clean Fresh Air, Easy Breathing;
Cool and Invigorate , Release Grief and Pain

If you feel like emotion is trapped in your lungs constricting your breathing, then this blend will help you release it.

Usage Tips:

- Apply to the chest or breathe in deeply from palms to clear airways and maintain easy breathing.
- Diffuse, inhale from palms/bottle or rub on chest/feet when environmental threats are high.
- Use when outdoors to minimize the effects of seasonal threats.
- Diffuse at bedtime to promote restful sleep.

Aromatic or Topical use only.

The scent of this blend reminds me of...

As you sit quietly, notice each breath you take.
Follow the intake of air with Respiratory blend
through your nose into your lungs and the slow
exhalation as you release the air through your
nose. Repeat this mindful breathing for several
minutes and notice how your body feels...

What do I want to breathe out (release); what do I want to breathe in (receive)?

Feeling grateful for the people in my life...

While inhaling Respiratory blend, think about the people in your life - family, friends etc, and let's draw some more circles.

Step 5b

Let each circle represent a person you love. While drawing each circle, think about your relationship with that person and the gratitude you feel to be sharing this life together. Reflect on what makes your relationship special. The circles could cross each other and be of different sizes. Let your hand lead and position the circles as you feel appropriate on the page. Draw as many circles as you want. You may even label them.

When you've finished with the circles, start drawing Neurolines from one end of the page to the other, going through the circles, "connecting" them into a web of love, gratitude and respect.

When you have drawn enough Neurolines, round the corners and you could even add colour.

What else am I grateful for?

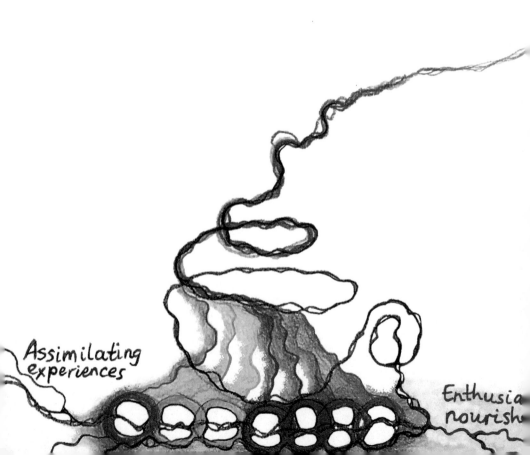

Assimilating
experiences

Enthusia
nourish

Digestzen
Digestive Blend

Peppermint, ~~Coriander,~~ Ginger, ~~Caraway,~~
~~Cardamom, Fennel, and Anise~~ essential oils.
Lemongrass

Healthy Digestive System;
Harmonizing Emotional Imbalances (which can contribute to an
upset stomach and digestive discomfort)

If you feel overwhelmed, overstimulated or overloaded
with information, if you could describe your state as
emotional indigestion, then this blend will assist in
assimilating and "digesting" life experiences.

Usage Tips:

- Add a few drops to water or tea and take internally to maintain
  healthy gastrointestinal tract.
- Rub on the stomach before flying or taking a road trip as part of
  a massage.
- Take it internally when traveling or trying new foods to soothe
  occasional stomach upset.
- Diffuse for a calming, sweet, minty aroma.

The scent of Digestive Blend reminds me of...

Sit quietly for a few moments with the
blend in the air and observe your thoughts
as they float by in your mind. Don't judge
them, just watch and notice.

What did you find out?
Would you like to write about it or draw?

What is causing me stress right now?

Did You Know: Essential oils are lipid soluble, which means they can usually travel through the walls of human cells. Many oils take effect in just 20min.

Aromatic Meditation

Take a few deep breaths inhaling
Digestive Blend and bring your
awareness inward. Simply relaxing
with your eyes closed allows you
to feel any unprocessed feelings
stored in the body. Staying with
your feelings with total loving
awareness lets emotions rise,
digest and fall away.

What did you discover in your
short meditation?

What I recently learned about myself is...

"You can have no dominion greater or less than that over yourself." Leonardo da Vinci

I could take better care of myself...

Do you prioritise your self-care or do you neglect your needs? Let's do some work on that, shall we?

You could start by drawing your self-care goals represented by circles. Allow your hand to draw freely, without over-thinking, as you position the circles around the page - bigger or smaller.

Then think about the reasons why you've chosen these goals and their benefits. With each thought that comes, draw a Neuroline that goes through the page, crossing the circles, joining everything together. The more lines you draw, the better and easier it will be to achieve the goals. Take notes as insights come to your mind while you're drawing.

Would you like to share in the community?

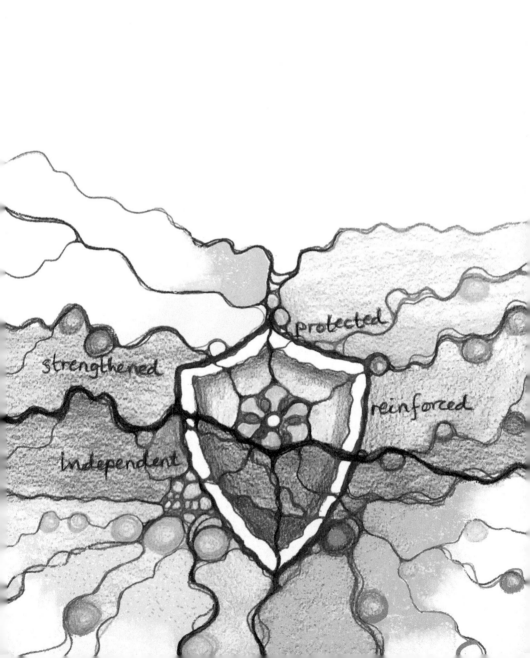

Protective Blend

~~Wild Orange Peel,~~ Clove Bud, ~~Cinnamon Leaf,~~ ~~Cinnamon Bark, Eucalyptus Leaf,~~ and ~~Rosemary~~ ~~Leaf/Flower~~ essential oils.

Grapefruit, Bergamot, Passion ♡

Protection against Environmental and Seasonal Threats; Strengthen Immune System; Strength to Say "NO!"

If you want to learn to stand up for yourself, be your authentic self and show up in integrity, then this blend can help.

Usage Tips:

- Take internally by adding two to three drops in a veggie capsule for immune support.
- Add to water for an effective all-purpose surface cleaner.
- Soak sliced apples in water and a few drops of Protective blend for a healthy, immune-supportive snack.
- Combine a few drops of the blend with fractionated coconut oil for a natural hand cleanser. (This is the liquid form of coconut oil).

When I smell Protective Blend I think of...

Sit quietly for a few moments with the blend
in the air and observe your thoughts as they
float by in your mind. Don't judge them, just
watch and notice.

What did you find out?
Would you like to write about it or draw?

I feel the strongest when...

It is hard to say NO to...

Make a list of everything you'd like to say "no" to.

How many of these are you currently doing?

It is hard to say YES to...

Make a list of everything you'd like to say "yes" to.

How many of these are you currently doing?

How do I embrace my true Self, even if it looks different from what others expect?

I am lovable and worthy of love.

"For, verily, great love springs from great knowledge of the beloved object, and if you little know it, you will be able to love it only little or not at all." Leonardo da Vinci

Goal Review

Look back at your Happiness Goals you set at the start of this Journal. Reflect on your experience: have you discovered something new about yourself or about the oils, have you had any insights or new realisations, or maybe your interest was sparked to learn how to use Neurographica drawing properly so you can begin to create and model your life according to your own plans, living life on your own terms?

As you go through your goals, be positive and encouraging.

It's absolutely fine if you didn't achieve all of your goals in such a short time. As your awareness expands, the way you perceive the oils and yourself will naturally change because you become a different person. In the words of Zig Ziglar, *"What you get by reaching your destination isn't nearly as important as who you become by reaching that destination".*

"Paradise is not a place. It is a state of consciousness."
Sri Chinmoy

Who is this new version of You?

Resources

Community

It is a lot easier and a lot more fun to journal alongside others. Our private Online community is the place to share insights and interesting discoveries, to help each other and encourage personal growth. This is your warm invitation to become a part of our vibrant community.

Art Studio

This is where you can find short video demonstrations of the Neurographica Steps. There are also longer video workshops on specific topics done with an instructor. This Online library is constantly growing with more resources being added regularly.

All you need to do is get a pen, some colouring pencils and use the last few blank pages in this journal to draw as you follow along. Check out *"My 3 Most Favourite Essential Oils"* video workshop which was specially created for this Happiness Journal. It is great fun and very enjoyable!

Happiness Gift Set

Happiness Journal makes an excellent present for a family member or a friend who loves deep thinking, essential oils and creativity. If you enjoyed using it, your loved ones would probably love having a copy of their own too.

If they don't have the 10 oils featured in the book, you can add them to your thoughtful gift by ordering the Happiness Gift Set.

All you need is this one link:

https://www.DesiStefanova.com/Journal

Further Reading

Emotions and Essential Oils, A Reference Guide for Emotional Healing, ISBN 978-1-7320281-8-0

Gifts of the Essential Oils, Explore the Wisdom, Lore and Spirit of the Plant Kingdom, ISBN 978-0-646-80776-8

About the Author

Desi Stefanova grew up in Bulgaria and discovered her love for herbs and art at a very young age but she only fully developed those interests after she had been on the path of personal development for a number of years and after moving to the UK.

A painful life event shook her to the core and made her re-evaluate her beliefs and perceptions about herself and the world around. Now Desi helps people to understand themselves better, to handle their emotions in an empowering way and she works with those who are ready to change their life by combining a variety of approaches: essential oils, PSYCH-K®, Neurographica® and others.

In 2020 Desi quit her long teaching career to follow her dreams of freedom, happiness and fulfillment.

Drop Desi an email at: *contact@DesiStefanova.com* to share how you are getting on with Happiness Journal or with any other questions or comments you may have.

Disclaimer

I, Desi, sincerely have the best intentions at heart and hope that this journal, the essential oils that go with it and Neurographica will manifest positivity and loving energy into your life, your mind, your body and your spirit.

I believe that pure essential oils and art complement other therapies and support our overall well-being as a part of holistic lifestyle.

Please note, this material is not intended to provide you with any specific health advice and should be used as a guide only.

For medical advice please consult a licensed health care professional.

Wishing you good health, wellbeing and personal growth,

Desi Stefanova

Book Review

THANK YOU

for your purchase of Happiness Journal. I hope it's proving helpful to you.

Happiness Journal came into existence in a very unusual way. Piece by piece of seemingly unrelated elements manifested themselves into my world and kept me puzzled for a while. I knew something was in the making but didn't know what until it was born. At one point all the pieces clicked into place and created a "manual" which takes you by the hand and leads you along a self-discovery path so that you can uncover what makes you trully happy. However, I had to learn quite a few new technical skills and grow as a person before I was able to present it to you in this form.

This is why I would really love to hear from you and appreciate your comments in the book review section of Amazon. These book reviews are very useful for both me as an author and the book itself so please do spare a minute to jot down a few words about your experience with Happiness Journal. Your opinion means a lot to me and I love reading every single one of the reviews I get. I look forward to reading yours!

Here are the quick links for your convenience (choose your local Amazon store):

For US, https://www.amazon.com/review/create-review?&asin=B0B188N1TB

For UK, https://www.amazon.co.uk/review/create-review?&asin=B0B188N1TBFor

Germany, https://www.amazon.de/review/create-review?&asin=B0B188N1TB

For France, https://www.amazon.fr/review/create-review?&asin=B0B188N1TB

For Spain, https://www.amazon.es/review/create-review?&asin=B0B188N1TB

For Italy, https://www.amazon.it/review/create-review?&asin=B0B188N1TB

For The Netherlands, https://www.amazon.nl/review/create-review?&asin=B0B188N1TB

For Canada, https://www.amazon.ca/review/create-review?&asin=B0B188N1TB

Thank You Again!

Printed in Great Britain
by Amazon

85340450R10059